The Playland Kids

Adventure book, in which a group of kids must summon help from a mighty recycler to overcome their obstacles so they can install a playland before the grand opening.

The Playland Kids

(Featuring Marcus Toussaint The Recycler)

Learn How to Recycle

Michael E. Toussaint Sr.
AUTHOR

Gotham Books
30 N Gould St.
Ste. 20820, Sheridan, WY 82801
https://gothambooksinc.com/
Phone: 1 (307) 464-7800

© 2023 Michael Toussaint. All rights reserved.
No part of this book may be reproduced, stored in
a retrieval system, or transmitted by any means without
the written permission of the author.

Published by Gotham Books (February 08, 2023)

ISBN: 979-8-88775-195-5 H
ISBN: 979-8-88775-189-4 P
ISBN: 979-8-88775-190-0 E

Any people depicted in stock imagery
provided by iStock are models, and such images
are being used for illustrative purposes only.

Certain stock imagery © iStock.

Because of the dynamic nature of the Internet, any web addresses,
or links contained in this book may have changed since
publication and may no longer be valid. The views expressed in
this work are solely those of the author and do not necessarily reflect the
views of the publisher, and the publisher hereby disclaims
any responsibility for them.

Dedication

This book is dedicated in memory of my oldest son,

Michael E Toussaint Jr.

publicly known as

Mustang Mike.

Close friends and Family called him Toot.

In 1990, he asked me what we all did when we go on the

road installing playlands.

I told him we did so much, I could write a book about it. He said,

" Why don't cha?" So I did.

The Playland Kids set out on another challenging journey. They had one day to install the Playland before the grand opening.

They were riding along a narrow winding road, when all of a sudden, Spit, quit, sputter, sounded the engine of their Playland Mobile.

"Oh no!" said Michael. "Not the engine again."

"What's wrong?" asked Mary Ann as she leaned over to hear the dreadful noise.

"We need water," said Michael. "Climbing up and down these hills drained all the water from the radiator."

"We just passed a service station about a mile back," said Gargle with a high-pitched gargling voice.

Jumping out of the Playland Mobile, Gargle and Buteye ran as fast as they could back to the station.

As they approached the self-service island, they saw the sign that read, "Sorry, we are out of gas and water."

"Oh no!" said Gargle. "What are we going to do now?"

Just then Gargle heard a roar just over the hill. Rrruh-em, rrrah-em, rrrah-em, sounded the big truck.

"Hey! I hear a big truck," said Gargle. "And it sounds like the water truck! It is! It is!"

The Blue Byrd Water truck roared over the hill with fresh water and gas. They filled their pails with water and raced back to the Playland Mobile as fast as they could.

Michael and the Playland Kids were very happy. They were back on the road again, singing and cheering.

IT PLAYS TO RECYCLE

MUSIC & LYRICS BY MICHAEL E. TOUSSAINT

IT PLAYS TO RE - CYCLE, IT PLAYS TO RE - CY - CLE -

1. pa - per cups and plastic too, we'll tell you just what to do
2. put them in a spe-cial bin - so - you can use them over - a - gain
3. pick them up from day to day - to - make a toy so you can play
4. so watch out for that spe-cial bin; IT PLAYS TO RE - CY - CLE!!!

But Michael was still a little worried. They had lost a lot of time and still had a long way to go. Just as they approached the next intersection, they saw a man waving a bright red flag. "Detour! Road closed," he shouted. "You have to go twenty miles that way."

"Oh no!" said Michael. "We'll never make it on time."

The Playland Kids were all getting worried. They were going in the wrong direction, and time was running out.

Meanwhile, back at The Playland Recycling Center, Marcus Toussaint, the Recycler, was hard at work. He had no idea that the Playland Kids were having any trouble.

It Plays To Recycle

He was busy stuffing the compactor recyclator with paper cups, paper bags, boxes, plastic cups, cans, newspapers, bottles, and all the recyclable material he could find.

It Plays To Recycle

Kling, klang! Boom! Sspat! Kling, klang! Boom! Sspat! sounded the big compactor recyclator as it spat out Playland parts by the thousands. Kling, klang! Boom! Sspat! Kling, klang! Boom! Sspat!

Back on the road, the Playland Kids were riding along, when all of a sudden they felt a big bump. They all bounced up and down on the seat again and again as the bump on the tire kept getting rougher and rougher and louder and louder! Kabunk! Kabunk! Kabunk! Kabunk!

Pow schrouge! Bang! Boom! Up went the back end of the Playland Mobile. Pling! Plang! Poof! All the Playland toys were all over the road.

"No, no, no!" said Michael. "Now we have a flat tire, and toys are everywhere. We'll never meet the deadline now."

"What are we going to do now?" Buteye asked nervously. "We're running out of time."

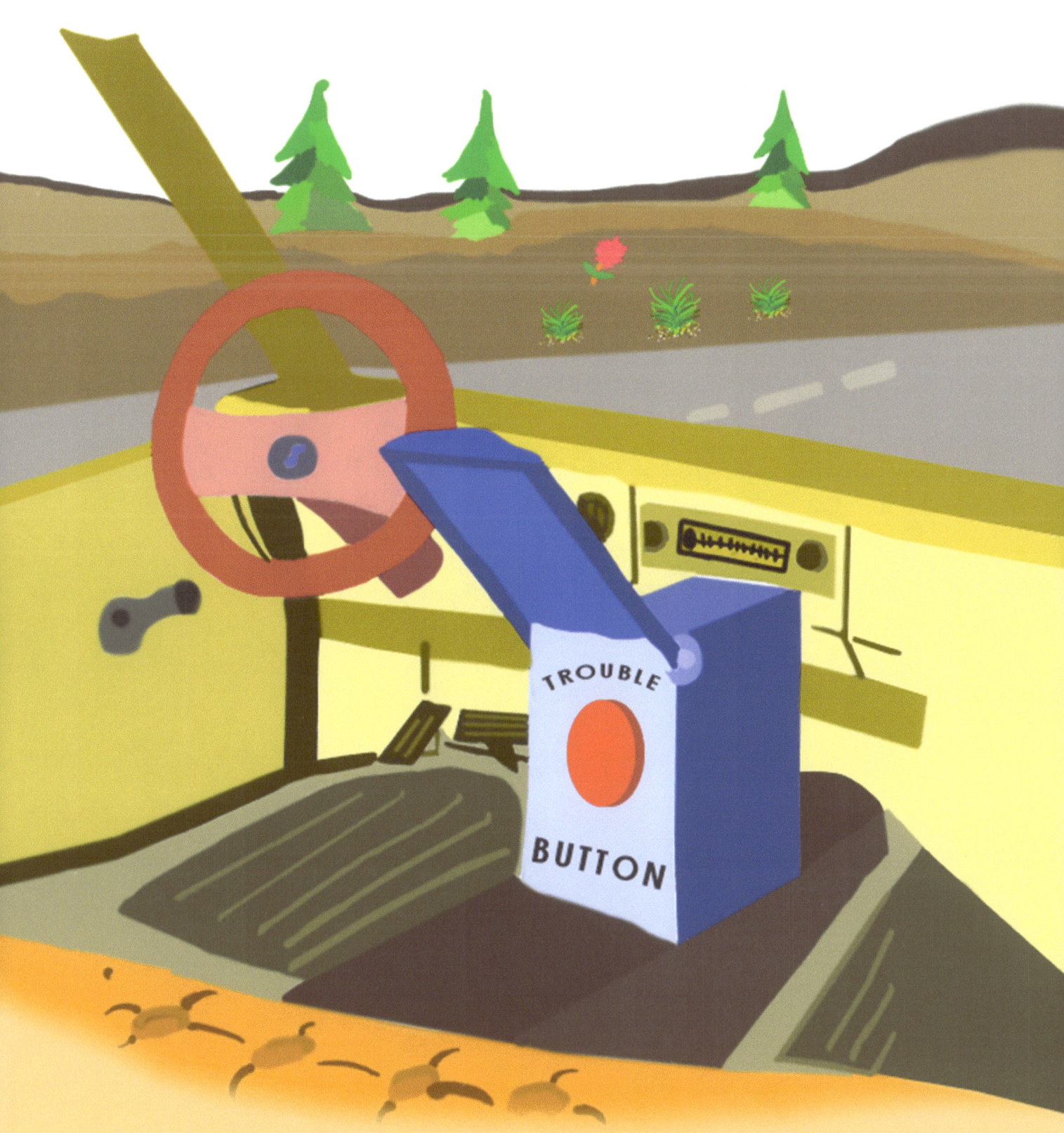

"I know," said Michael. "Looks like we're going to have to call ... Marcus Toussaint, the Recycler." Michael unlocked the special box on the console of the Playland Mobile and pushed the trouble button.

Back at the Playland Recycling Center, the trouble alarm went off: "Trouble! Trouble!"

Marcus Toussaint, the Recycler, heard the alarm. "Oh no! The Playland Kids are in trouble," he said.

Marcus Toussaint, the Recycler, went into a secret room and shouted the code words-"It plays to recycle!"

Whiss! Zzapp! Blam buckle! The big compactor recyclator opened its doors, and out came the jet mobile, a computerized recycling machine with two jet engines and an instant Playland toy maker in the rear.

Marcus Toussaint, the Recycler, jumped into his jet mobile and roared down the highway. Ssszzzooommm!

Moments later, Mary Ann looked up and shouted, "Here he comes! Look, everybody! Look!"

The Playland Kids were jumping and shouting with joy. "Yay, Marcus! Yay, Marcus!"

The Playland Kids got into the jet mobile and zzoooomed on to the Playland store.

The Playland Kids took all the plastic, cans, bottles, and paper from the special recycling bin and put the materials in the instany recycling machine. Kling, klang! Boom! Sspat! Out came parts for the new Playland.

The Playland toys were finished for the grand opening, and all the kids were happy.

Marcus Toussaint, the Recycler, turned around and said, "Don't forget, boys and girls, it plays to recycle!"

The Recycler is off to save the day again!

Hey, boys and girls. Do you know how to recycle?

It seems that my friends have forgotten how to recycle.

I have to call the Recycler for help.

Recycling is one of the most important things a hero can do to save the planet. There are more than ten million recycling heroes on the planet.

Are you one of them? Do you know what to recycle and what to throw in the trash?

Bring your old cell phone back to your local phone store. They will recycle it and turn it into a new phone.

Aluminum cans are 100 percent recyclable! You can recycle them over and over again, making new cans out of old cans.

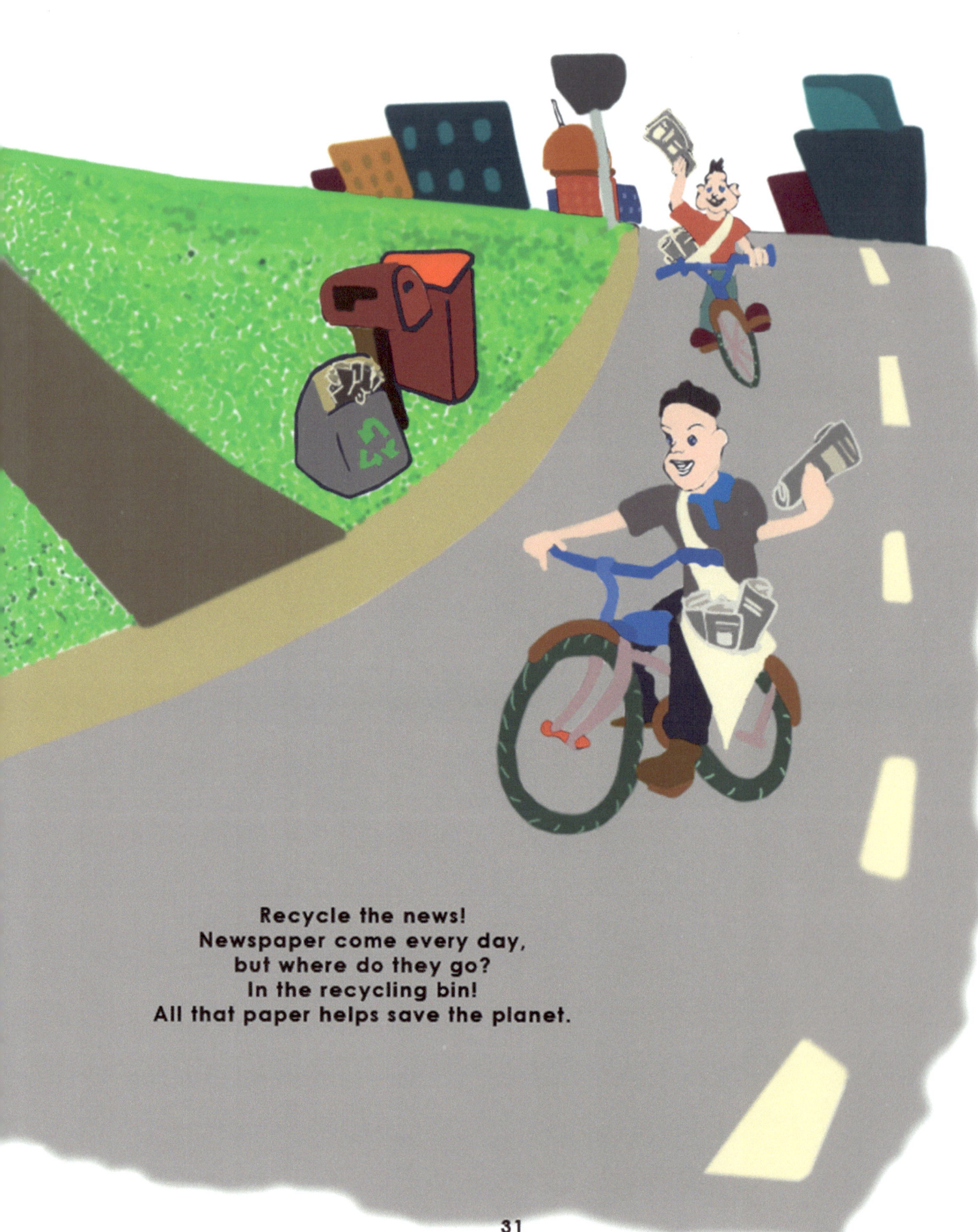

Recycle the news!
Newspaper come every day,
but where do they go?
In the recycling bin!
All that paper helps save the planet.

All your magazines are recyclable! Why not recycle your magazines? It saves power, tress, and water!

The plastic bottles that hold your bleach, shampoo, milk, water, and even soap are recyclable too! Make sure you clean and rinse them out before putting them in the recycling bin.

Plastic bottle caps are made with a different plastic. You have to put the caps in a separate bin when you recycle them.

You cannot recycle your juice boxes! The cardboard is not the right kind.

Make sure you ask a parent or another grown-up to help you with glass bottles. Broken glass is very sharp and dangerous.

Connect the dots.

Seems like Marcus has lost his edges!
Will you help him connect the dots?

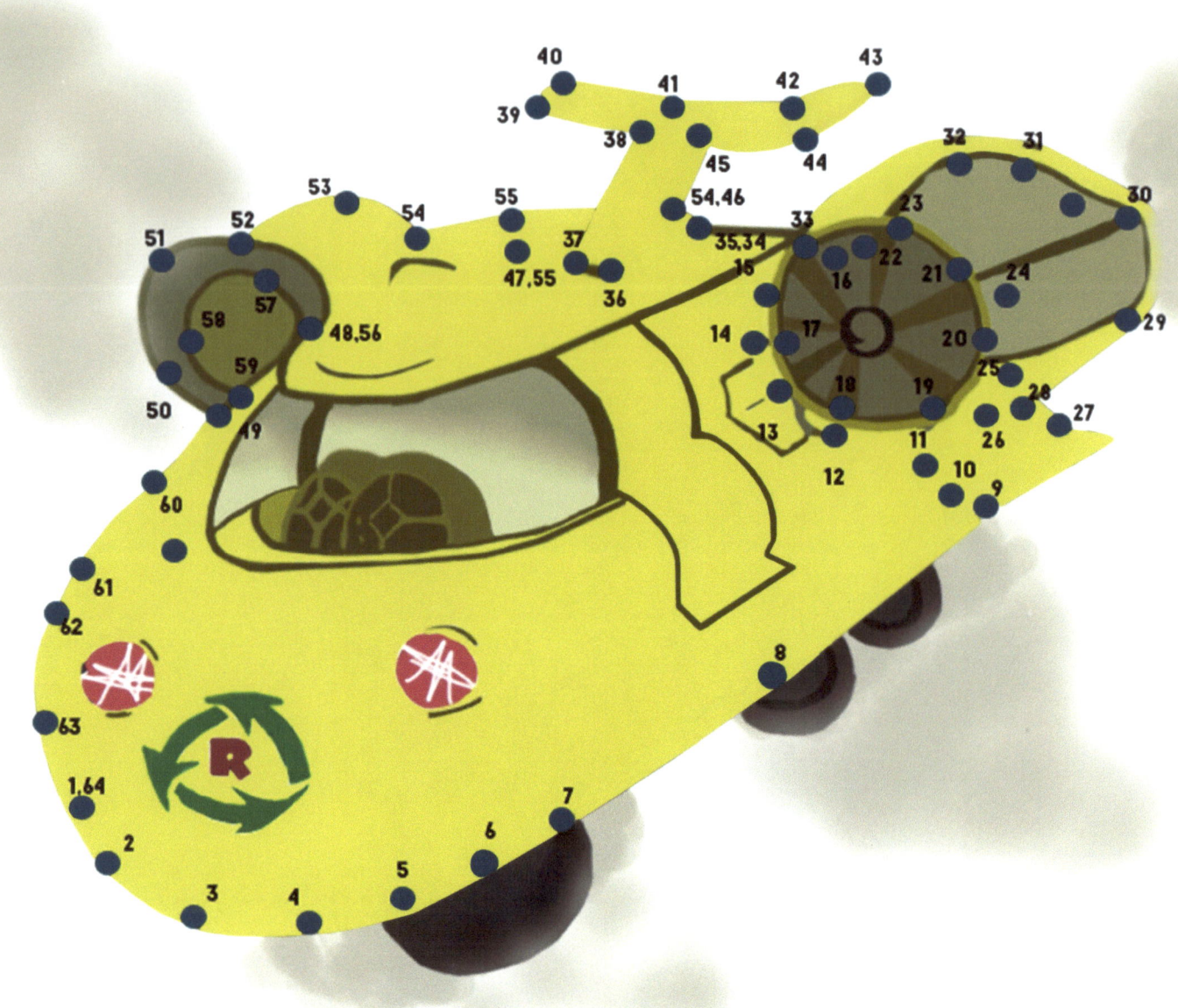

Is that the Recycler's Rocket?

Coffee cups are not recyclable. You can reuse them by turning them into flowerpots.

Put your old food in a compost bin. Worms eat your old food and turn it into garden soil.

Cardboard boxes are recyclable too! Bring your old cardboard to be recycled, and turn it into new cardboard.

You can bring all your recycled cans, bottles, plastic containers, and newspapers to your school to be recycled. Ask your teacher about starting a recycling project.

When you are through surfing the web on your old computer, you can recycle the computer or give it to a friend in need.

You can't recycle your food boxes! Once there is food on the box, it cannot be recycled.

It's raining paper! Shredded paper cannot be recycled!

Wire hangers can break the recycling machines. Bring them to your local dry cleaners instead of throwing them away!

Batteries poison the ground when you throw them in the trash. Buy rechargeable batteries to help save the earth!

You can recycle aluminum cans, cars, washers, dryers, and dishwashers. Call the Recycler to scoop them up and take them away!

You can turn in your old sheets, shoes, and clothes to thrift stores. They will give them to the homeless at the shelter. Give your old blankets to animal shelters, as blankets help keep small animals warm during the winter.

**Help the Recycler out!
There are plenty of things to do in your
town that can save the planet!**

At the Recycling Center they will take everything you recycle and turn them into
new toys!

Thank you, Recycler, for teaching my friends how to recycle!

The Recycler is off to save the planet!
Until the next time!
"It plays to recycle. Goodbye recycling friends."

www.ingramcontent.com/pod-product-compliance
Lightning Source LLC
LaVergne TN
LVHW070438070526
838199LV00036B/665